INSTANT
TIME MANAGEMENT

Instant Time Management

The INSTANT-Series *Presents*

INSTANT

TIME MANAGEMENT

How to Manage Time and Get More Done Faster Instantly!

Instant Series Publication

Copyright © Instant Series Publication

All rights reserved.

It is impermissible to reproduce any part of this book without prior consent. All violations will be prosecuted to the fullest extent of the law.

While attempts have been made to verify the information contained within this publication, neither the author nor the publisher assumes any responsibility for errors, omissions, interpretation or usage of the subject matter herein.

This publication contains the opinions and ideas of its author and is intended for informational purpose only. The author and publisher shall in no even held liable for any loss or other damages incurred from the usage of this publication.

ISBN 978-1-511-40411-2

Printed in the United States of America

First Edition

FIRST STEP:

Before proceeding, visit http://www.instantseries.com, and join the **INSTANT Newsletter** now.

You will want to! :)

Instant Time Management

CONTENTS

Chapter 1 - Benefits of Effective Time Management

13 - "If Only I Had More Time!"

14 - What Is Time Management

15 - All About Progression

16 - Why Organize Yourself

18 - Exercise: Assess Your Organization

Chapter 2 - Tools for Effective Time Management

23 - Time Management Tools

24 - How To Use Your Tools

27 - Exercise: Apply Your Tools

Chapter 3 - Steps in Effective Time Management

29 - All In The Plans

31 - Planning In Action

35 - Long-Term Time Management

40 - Exercise: Plan Your Daily And Weekly Activities

Chapter 4 - Implementation of Time for Effective Time Management

41 - Deadlines And Specificities Are Your Friends

42 - Break Things Up With Allocated Times

44 - Timing Tasks

46 - Exercise: Time Yourself

Chapter 5 - Timing Your Activities for Effective Time Management

48 - Advanced Scheduling

50 - Incorporate Color Coding And Audio Reminders

53 - Pinpoint Your Optimal Work Time

57 - Have A One-Year Advance

60 - Exercise: Start Smart Scheduling

Chapter 6 - Evaluating the Effectiveness of Your Time Management

62 - Measure Your Effectiveness

63 - To Know If Progressing Or Not

64 - Exercise: Divide And Evaluate

Chapter 7 - Optimizing Difficult Tasks in Your Schedule for Effective Time Management

66 - Check Off Or Cross Off

67 - Live To Fight Another Die

68 - Exercise: Reschedule Optimization

Chapter 8 - Daily Nightly Habits for Effective time Management

70 - Plan Your Next Day

71 - You Are the Boss And Assistant

72 - Exercise: Daily Progress Equates Yearly Success

Chapter 9 - Exercises for Effective time Management

74 - Exercise 1: Test Your Understanding

75 - Exercise 2: Create Your Schedules

76 - Exercise 3: Assimilate All The Tools

77 - Exercise 4: Synergize What Works

Chapter 10 - No Tasks Left Behind for Effective Time Management

78 - Follow Through Your Schedule

79 - Time Management Chart

82 - Implementation Table

84 - Exercise: Use Last Minute Chart

Chapter 11 - The Time to Start Effective Time Management is NOW

86 - More Times Are Wasted Than Ever

87 - Time Management Is Just Self-Management

Instant Time Management

Instant Time Management

Chapter 1
Benefits of Effective Time Management

"If Only I Had More Time!"

You've certainly said that phrase at one or maybe several points in your life while frustratingly beating your head against the wall or pulling your hair out. Maybe you're saying to yourself, "*IF* only I had more time" or "I wish I could go back in time and get this done faster!"

Well, don't worry. You're not the only one who has these moments of regret. Everybody goes through them, from time to time.

The reason you can't get anything done throughout the day, the week, or even the year is most likely a problem of *managing your time properly.* Or perhaps, you don't know what **time management** is.

What Is Time Management

It's never too late to pick up on what you're lacking because time management is really a simple concept that relies simply on organization and then sticking to it.

- To make it more palpable, think of yourself of the manager of your daily routine. By being the manager, you are required to get things moving during a pre-determined frame of time.

- Think of yourself as a contractor who has just won a project, as well as the field manager, whose job on site is to manage workers. You keep everybody on track so that the project can be completed on time and the final payment from the client can be paid in full, without any deductions justified by any delay in completion.

Overall, time management is what allows things to get done more effectively. At the end of the day, it helps you accomplish things.

All About Progression

Technically speaking, everything revolves around **ideals** and **goals**; whatever you do, it is best to move forward.

For instance, if you're a school teacher, you might like to be the principal eventually when it's all said and done, or maybe you hope to marry the person you love one day.

Thus, everything is about *moving forward*. For you to move forward, you need your life to be more organized. To be more precise, you need to have better organization of your time during the day or the week.

Whether it's something you want to achieve in a day or 5 years from now, you need to plan ahead, and work according to a chosen time frame.

Why Organize Yourself

If you are naturally lazy and don't feel like being dynamic when it comes to organizing more time to go through your daily routines, now is the time to start doing things the right way. You will have nothing to lose. You will only to gain benefits that will make your life simpler and more enjoyable.

In other words, when opting for effective time management you will:

1. Do things on time that will enable you to move forward. In other words, with proper planning of your day, you allow yourself to allocate defined activities to a

certain time frame, you will work faster to move to the next tasks in order to get more done

2. Learn how to organize yourself a bit better. Nothing is more beneficial than, setting up a schedule, with exactly what to do, and at what time you must get into action.

3. Stick to the essentials and you will more easily get things done. By sticking to your plan, you are sticking to what matters, instead of trying desperately to remember what to do, the answer is right there in front of your eyes, like writing in plain sight, shall we say. This enables you to save time and work faster.

4. Reach your objectives faster by sticking to the plan. Organization - by respecting your chosen timing- is a good supporting tool for your objectives.

5. Have a better idea of your daily activities or routine. People have so many things to do, or they just have no clue on how to keep up with a plan.

What to keep in mind here is that time management depends entirely on *how you organize* YOURSELF. The word "organizing" might be vague to you, but it will be explained further later.

Exercise: Assess Your Organization

Do the following exercise.

How organized are you? Choose the **most accurate answers**.

1.) When you wake up in the morning, what is your routine when you get out of bed?
   a.) Brush your teeth, make your bed, take a shower, get dressed, verify that you are not forgetting anything, and then leave for work/school.

b.) Smoke a cigarette, have a glass of water, read a few lines in the papers, get dressed quickly, get out of the house. Then, halfway to your destination you realize that you've omitted doing or taking certain things, like brushing your teeth or an important file.

c.) Brush your teeth, take a shower, get dressed, have breakfast quickly, prepare what you need for the day (in terms of work files, or laptop, books, *etc.*), and then you leave the house for your destination.

2.) When writing an exam, what do you do first?

a.) You read the questions first, evaluate the amount of time you have to complete your test, and then start working.

b.) You look for the easy questions first, answer them first, and then carry on with the rest of your test.

c.) Read the questions first, write down whatever information you remember, then start with the questions that are the easiest

3.) When handling your tasks at home, what is a typical Saturday to you?

a.) Clean-up is in the morning, lunch is scheduled for 1 p.m., afternoons are for grocery shopping, and night time for leisure.

b.) You eat breakfast first and discuss politics, you think about where to have lunch around 2 p.m., at 4 p.m. you take a nap, at 6 p.m. you plan the rest of the evening with friends.

c.) You clean-up in the mornings at least until 10 a.m., eat breakfast, cook lunch for 12:30 p.m., in the afternoon you think about grocery shopping for the house, evenings are normally dedicated for family and friends.

*If you've mostly chosen **answer A**, *congratulations*, you are the type who works according to a certain methodology. You get things done the traditional way - with dedication. You are not the type to abandon the way you do things easily because it works for you. You should now learn to make your organization process even more effective and exciting by adding more tools and methods to this process.

If you've mostly chosen **answer B, *sorry to say*, you are not very good at managing your time. You've got little to no organization, no focus and you probably lose or forget things, such as files for work or your phone, for the simple reason that you don't remember where you've left them. You personally feel like there's never enough time to do anything and often wonder how other people do it. You should find a way to put things in order from now on, otherwise you will continue to feel that you never get much done in life.

***If you've mostly chosen **answer C**, you are a control freak, everything has to be put in order otherwise you're not happy. You work with a schedule every day and everyone around you must abide by it. But you should stop being rigid, because being inflexible can be overwhelming when there can be a better way. Introduce a couple of organization tools so that you can plan your routine or objectives by using "time" the right way.

<u>Chapter 2</u>

Tools for Effective Time Management

Time Management Tools

To get started, think about what you are going to use to organize YOURSELF. Your time needs to be planned in advanced everyday if you want to manage it better. Therefore, it is important that you arm yourself with the necessary tools.

You should have the appropriate tools to write down your schedule for the day, week, month or year, so you'll need an **organizer** – either in paper or electronic form, whatever suits you. You should carry it with you every day and everywhere, as you need to keep up with your schedule and make sure you are respecting the time frames you've chosen.

Next, you need to set a **reminder**. A reminder can be an alarm, it can even be in musical form. In other words, you'll need to set a timer which will serve as an alarm that will be supported by sound (music, ring tone), and make sure each activity has its own ring tone.

A reminder can also be color coded. A color code helps you differentiate different activities, during the day by choosing a color for the different hours in the day for instance. Or you can choose to color code by week by allocating a color to each week. The same can be applied to monthly planning or yearly planning for these long-term objectives.

How To Use Your Tools

Let's go through the following <u>example</u> together, so that you can have a better understanding here.

Let's say that you are a wedding planner and you have to start working on a client's wedding preparation for the next day. You have been solicited to organize a "dream wedding" for a new client; she is very demanding, and wants something extraordinary.

In order to be professional, you have to organize yourself first, to avoid collateral damage in the future. Organizing means knowing what needs to be done, because, let's not forget, that your job is to be a professional.

So what do you do first? You use your **organizing tool**, and:

1.) *Write down* whatever needs to be done. Keeping the example of the wedding planner in mind, you need to order the items, set the tables at the wedding venue, set an appointment for the cake and bring the decorator to the venue for decoration.

2.) Then, you *evaluate the total time* needed to complete the whole task and downsize it into small-sized bites for each activity. Use the following as an example: order tables and chairs at 10:30 a.m., get the costs 5 minutes later (10:35 a.m.), get the chairs and tables to the wedding venue delivered by 12:00 p.m., set your cake appointment for 40 minutes after the chairs and tables are delivered, and finally set the time when you should meet the decorator at the wedding venue 90 minutes after you get to the cake appointment with your client.

3.) Now, you can *use your reminders*. If you choose an alarm or a sound reminder, you can set each time-set to an alarm sound or a ring tone. If you opt for color coding, each time-set should correspond to a certain color. For instance, the activity set for 10:30 a.m. can be written in *red*, the one in 10:35 a.m. in *black*, and son on (you can also use highlighters of different colors).

4.) Lastly, *consult your schedule* by reading it through once.

Note that time-setting consists of choosing a realistic time frame in which you will have enough time to complete a task - meaning that if you feel an activity should last three hours, don't set it for an hour. You will learn how to use color coding and other reminders throughout your day later. Don't forget that they are applicable for everyday activities and long-term objectives.

<u>Exercise</u>: Apply Your Tools

Here's an <u>activity</u> for you.

1.) Write down your routine (*or type it, whatever works for you*) for the day.

2.) Choose a reminder that best suits you (sound or color).

3.) Exercise on how you can manage your time effectively throughout the day by setting a ring tone on your mobile phone corresponding to each new activity and set at a precise hour of the day. Do the same thing with color coding (each activity, written in different color or underlined or highlighted with a different color).

- Which reminder is more effective? Explain

- Do you feel that, color coding works better for short term activities? Explain.

Now, let's move on to the next chapter, with a more detailed explanation on how to manage your time more effectively.

Chapter 3

Steps in Effective Time Management

All In The Plans

Effective management of your **time** comes with *effective planning* of your **routine** around a certain portion of your time.

First you have to <u>write down</u> whatever needs to be done. If it's about a daily routine, regroup all your activities and write them *down/type* in your organizer (paper or electronic format). Do the same with your weekly planning, your monthly planning, and your yearly planning. But always start at the bottom, your daily routine.

If you are planning to buy an expensive TV by the end of the year, start by managing your time working towards achieving that goal on a <u>daily basis</u> first.

So the planning methodology for time management works the following way:

1.) First, you regroup you daily activities. List them down, and make an accurate description or comment next to each activity.

2.) Rank them. Here, you should choose which one is a priority, which ones should be done during the day or the afternoon, etc. Make a list with headings (priorities, evening, morning, home, etc.)

3.) Then rank them according to importance by writing down a number next to each categories (1, 2, 3, 4, etc.).

Overall, this is how you should manage your time daily. First regroup your activities by making a description of each one of them (this will help you rank them easier), then you should decide which should be a priority and then you should make a final ranking. This is a sort of schedule, or the premise to setting a schedule. *And who hasn't heard about schedules?*

Planning In Action

Let's work through the following example before moving on.

Imagine that you have to organize a fundraiser for your university. The fundraiser's purpose will be for an association that you started with friends to help save rubber back turtles on the coasts of Central West Africa.

Now you can only imagine all the activities that have to be put together to plan a successful event, not to mention the strategies you have to come up with to convince people to donate enough money for your cause.

For an event to be successful, you have to get organized, and being organized means essentially, to come up with a plan. So planning, in this instance, is essential. Let's now have a look on how you will proceed.

1.) First, write down all that needs to be done to organize a fundraiser. Write down the steps to follow, the venues needed, the expenses, the people needed to be contacted, *etc.*, together with what needs to be done for the day, like this:

> *Pay the rent*
> *elaborate lists of guests for the fundraising,*
> *make calls for different venues and get the costs*
> *Lunch*
> *Get little sister from school*
> *History Class at 10h30 for 1h30 hours*
> *15 minutes break*
> *Applied economics class at 14h30 for 2hours*
> *Workout*
> *Call mom*
> *Go to the library to get the book on contemporary art*
> *Have to watch the latest news at 7h00pm*
> *Dinner*
> *Go to bed*

2.) The second step, would be to organize them in order of importance (or a hierarchy of value), and writing a description or comment next to it, and ranking them using headings.

Fundraising activities
-Elaborate lists of guests for the fundraising,(at least 100 for today)
-make calls for different venues and get the costs(target is at least 10 venues)

School schedule for the day
-History Class at 10h30 for 1h30 hours
-15 minutes break(need to answer those e-mails)
-Applied economics class at 14h30 for 2hours
-Go to the library to get the book on contemporary art
-Lunch

Home
-Pay the rent
-Get little sister from school(she finishes school at 5h00)
-Workout
-Call mom(she's very sick)
-Have to watch the latest news at 7h00pm(important)
-Eat Dinner
-Go to bed

3.) Then, finally rank them by writing a number next to each list.

Fundraising activities (1)
-Elaborate lists of guests for the fundraising,(at least 100 for today)
-make calls for different venues and get the costs(target is at least 10 venues)

School schedule for the day (2)
-History Class at 10h30 for 1h30 hours
-15 minutes break(need to answer those e-mails)
-Applied economics class at 14h30 for 2hours
-Go to the library to get the book on contemporary art
-Lunch

Home (3)
-Pay the rent
-Get little sister from school(she finishes school at 5h00)
-Workout
-Call mom(she's very sick)
-Have to watch the latest news at 7h00pm(important)
-Eat Dinner
-Go to bed

So, you've managed to set up an organized schedule or plan by identifying your priorities. To be more precise, in this example you are supposed to find a way to manage your time to accomplish all these things during the day.

- Let's also add in that time management, is not only about having things done, but also having them done on time, so that you don't end up wishing that you had more time to do more. This is why the *fundraiser* is the **number one priority** in our example. It's something you rarely do and therefore you can't really postpone it because the event attendee you need will not always be available.

- Then you have the **second priority**, *school schedule*. School is not about having a good time, it's mostly about hard work and focus. Furthermore, you only have 4 years (more or less) to graduate, so you might as well rank it high in your list of priorities.

- Lastly, you have the *activities pertaining to your home*, it is **last on your list** simply because you can rely on others when you lack time to pay the rent or a workout session can always be moved to Saturday morning for example.

It is important to prioritize the activities that demand a lot of effort.

Long-Term Time Management

Now, let's see how planning works when it comes to projects that are longer.

Imagine that the fundraising is set at the end of the month, and that you plan on inviting politicians, actors and the media.

Here's an example of the different steps to follow:

<u>Step 1</u>: Write down all your activities for the week/month. Write down your general activities. There will be gaps when you set up your schedule, but anticipate with what you know you will be doing for the next 4 weeks, apart from the activities around the fundraising.

Pay the rent once a month
Elaborate lists of guests for the fundraising
Make calls for different venues and get the costs
Set up an appointment for those personalities that are hard to reach
Set up a list of whatever will be needed for the event (tables, chairs, drinks etc...)
See what's needed for the cocktail after presentation of the project.
Lunch
Get little sister from school every day after school
Class at 10h30 for 1h30 hours
15 minutes break every day after first class
Second class at 14h30 for 2hours
Workout 4 times a week
Time out, when I can make all my important calls
Go to the library for studying time or borrowing a book
Watch TV for 2 hours after getting home.
Dinner
Go to bed

Step 2: Rank your activities in terms of importance.

<u>Fundraising activities</u>(must have completed at least 3 out of 4 activities)
Elaborate lists of guests for the fundraising
Make calls for different venues and get the costs
Set up an appointment for those personalities that are hard to reach
Set up a list of whatever will be needed for the event (tables, chairs, drinks etc...)
See what's needed for the cocktail after presentation of the project.

<u>School</u>(my classmate will join me for lunch sometimes)
Lunch
Class at 10h30 for 1h30 hours
15 minutes break every day after first class
Second class at 14h30 for 2hours
Go to the library for studying time or borrowing a book

<u>Home</u>(Must try not to miss any workout session)
Pay the rent once a month
Get little sister from school every day after school
Workout 4 times a week
Time out, when I can make all my important calls
Watch TV for 2 hours after getting home
Dinner
Go to bed

Here, the comments are directly written next to the heading. This could be done for long lists, but you can also opt for writing a comment or a description next to an activity on your list.

Step 3: Ranking with numbers, it's the same principle as your daily planning, where you should prioritize the things that are harder to achieve or harder to control, like other people's availability, or time (you won't be a student forever).

(1)

Fundraising activities (must have completed at least 3 out of 4 activities)
Elaborate lists of guests for the fundraising
Make calls for different venues and get the costs
Set up an appointment for those personalities that are hard to reach
Set up a list of whatever will be needed for the event (tables, chairs, drinks etc...)
See what's needed for the cocktail after presentation of the project.

School (my classmate will join me for lunch sometimes)
Lunch
Class at 10h30 for 1h30 hours (2)
15 minutes break every day after first class
Second class at 14h30 for 2hours
Go to the library for studying time or borrowing a book

Home (Must try not to miss any workout session) (3)
Pay the rent once a month
Get little sister from school every day after school
Workout 4 times a week
Time out, when I can make all my important calls
Watch TV for 2 hours after getting home
Dinner
Go to bed

You can even add in a <u>Step 4</u>, with color coding already inserted in the process.

(1)

Fundraising activities(must have completed at least 3 out of 4 activities)
Elaborate lists of guests for the fundraising
Make calls for different venues and get the costs
Set up an appointment for those personalities that are hard to reach
Set up a list of whatever will be needed for the event (tables, chairs, drinks etc...)
See what's needed for the cocktail after presentation of the project.

School(my classmate will join me for lunch sometimes)
Lunch
Class at 10h30 for 1h30 hours (2)
15 minutes break every day after first class
Second class at 14h30 for 2hours
Go to the library for studying time or borrowing a book

Home(Must try not to miss any workout session) (3)
Pay the rent once a month
Get little sister from school every day after school
Workout 4 times a week
Time out, when I can make all my important calls
Watch TV for 2 hours after getting home
Dinner
Go to bed

Color coding here, will help you differentiate the prioritized activities from the normal ones.

Color coding is perfect in the planning process because it captures immediately your attention when you consult your schedule for the week, or the day. It can also help in grabbing your attention for what is to come during the year if you are able to plan that far in advanced. You can use any color you wish for color coding.

Note that you can also use color coding for your daily activities, especially when you have too many things to do at a time.

<u>Exercise</u>: Plan Your Daily And Weekly Activities

Do the following exercise.

1.) On a piece of paper, organize your **daily activities**, by writing them down (all of them).

2.) Next, rank them by order of importance (follow the guideline).

3.) Do the same exercise with your **weekly activities**. Use *color coding* this time as the 4th step.

Chapter 4
Implementation of Time for Effective Time Management

Deadlines And Specificities Are Your Friends

Now that you've gone through smart planning, let's move on to the next step which is timing during implementation.

Since you are the time manager of your own schedule (activities during the day, weeks, and so on), you should be able to evaluate proper timing for each of these activities.

This will, help you make your planning more concrete, because quantifying an activity with timing will help you complete it more effectively.

For example, let's say that you give yourself **7 minutes** to clean your 50-inch TV by **10 a.m.** This will result in you doing it MORE EFFECTIVELY than if you just tell yourself broadly *"this TV needs to be cleaned today."*

Let's be honest, you'll probably forget about it after 5 minutes; however, if you've set yourself a time to start wiping the TV, and the duration needed to do it, your TV is more likely to be cleaned up at the end of the day.

Specificity is key.

Break Things Up With Allocated Times

- So the first step in setting a realistic timing for implementation, is to set up a time when you want to start your activity.

- After that, evaluate how much time you need to accomplish this task.

- Try to be as brief as possible. Set it for a minimum of *10-to-20 minutes* and maximum of *30 minutes-to-1 hour* for technical tasks (manual work, reports, number of chapters to read, *etc.*) and *4-to-5 hours* for non-technical tasks (like creative writing).

If for instance, you've planned on doing some researches on how to invest in stock exchange at 10 a.m., give it a *maximum 1 hour* by dividing your search in <u>different categories</u> like:

- What is stock investment? *(15 minutes research)*, you should set an audio reminder at the end of the first 15 minutes

- How does it work? *(15 minutes research)*, second audio reminder (ring tone) at the end of the second 15 minutes search.

- How do you become successful? *(15 minutes research)*, third audio reminder at the end of the third 15 minutes search

- When can you claim your money? *(15 minutes research)*, final audio reminder at the end of the last 15 minutes search.

Right here, not only have you rendered your activity more practical by defining it and dividing it into 4 questions that will help you with your research, but you are also better managing your 1 hour of research this way and being resourceful with your time.

Timing Tasks

Lets' see with another example. This time, you want to practice singing a song you want to record at the end of the week. So you've set your practice session at around 4 o'clock in the afternoon, give it a maximum 4 hours.

Here's how you will manage your 4-hour rehearsal:

1.) First, you warm up your voice for 20 minutes (left with 3 hours 40 minutes). Use your alarm (on vibrate), to signal the end of the 20 minutes.

2.) Second, start singing to the music (try for one hour, 2 hours 40 minutes left). Use the alarm (on vibrate), to signal the end of the one hour.

3.) Third, sing without the music twice (try for 1 hour, 1 hour 40 minutes left). Use the alarm (on vibrate), to signal the end of the one hour.

4.) Fourth, sing again with the music (for an hour, 40minutes left). Use the alarm (on vibrate), to signal the end of the hour.

5.) Fifth, clear you voice with some water for 5 minutes, and for the remaining 35 minutes, practice singing with the music again. Use the alarm as a ringtone after the first 5 minutes, and on vibrate mode after the last 35 minutes.

Exercise: Time Yourself

Do the following exercise.

1.) Choose an activity (a random one), that you normally do (pick one that is long enough for this exercise)

2.) Try to downsize the activity in small segments and write down these small segments, if you prefer.

3.) Assign a time of implementation for each segment. At the end of each implementation, assign a ringtone.

- Is it more practical to organize your activity in that manner? Explain.

- Are the ringtones really helpful? Explain.

Chapter 5
Timing Your Activities for Effective Time Management

Advanced Scheduling

The next step helps you decide when (at what time) an activity should be started.

- You've first elaborated a plan, identified your priority, now it's the time to set the implementation process by assigning each activity to a time slot. Priorities comes first, followed by the list ranked second after those priorities.

If we consider the previous example, the schedule with an allocated time slot, it should look as followed:

Monday 01-20-2015

8-00	-Elaborate lists of guests for the fundraising
8-30	-Make calls for different venues and get the costs
9-00	-Set up an appointment for those personalities that are hard to reach
9-30	-Set up a list of whatever will be needed for the event
10-00	-See what's needed for the cocktail after presentation of the project.
10-30	-Class at for 1h30 hours
11-00	--
11-30	--
12-00	-15 minutes break after the class(pay the rent)
12-30	-Lunch
13-00	--
13-30	--
14-00	-Second class for 2 hours
14-30	--
15-00	--
15-30	--
16-00	-Go to library for studying or borrowing a book.
16-30	-Get little sister from school
17-00	-Call mom
17-30	-Workout
18-00	--
18-30	--
19-00	Watch the news at 7
19-30	--
20-00	-Dinner
20-30	--
21-00	-Go to bed
21-30	--
22-00	

Incorporate Color Coding And Audio Reminders

Now let's see how we can use color coding or audio reminders in here.

Let's start with color coding. Color coding in here is supposed to tell you in which category each color belongs to.

For example, if you've chosen **red** for activities around the fundraising event, **grey** for house activities, and **blue** for school, color coding is supposed to tell you which is which at a glance when you consult your organizer.

So color coding on your organizer should be used as follows:

Instant Time Management

Monday 01-20-2015

```
8-00    -Elaborate lists of guests for the fundraising
8-30    -Make calls for different venues and get the costs
9-00    -Set up an appointment for those personalities that are hard to reach
9-30    -Set up a list of whatever will be needed for the event
10-00   -See what's needed for the cocktail after presentation of the project.
10-30   -Class at for 1h30 hours
11-00   ............................................................
11-30   ............................................................
12-00   -15 minutes break after the class(pay the rent)
12-30   -Lunch
13-00   ............................................................
13-30   ............................................................
14-00   -Second class for 2 hours
14-30   ------------------------------------------------------------
15-00   ............................................................
15-30   ............................................................
16-00   -Go to library for studying or borrowing a book.
16-30   -Get little sister from school
17-00   -Call mom
17-30   -Workout
18-00   ............................................................
18-30   ............................................................
19-00   Watch the news at 7
19-30   ............................................................
20-00   -Dinner
20-30   ............................................................
21-00   -Go to bed
21-30   ............................................................
22-00
```

Do you see how color coding, helps you differentiate between different categories (school, event, home)?

- It is a very practical reminder and helps you determine what to do immediately, such as after finding out what's needed for the cocktail scheduled for the event (in red) at 10 a.m.

- Then you see the color blue right after this line, and you know it's a school activity that follows.

- Right in the middle of the blue lines, you see one line in grey, reminding you that you have to take care of something at home; and as you go on within your schedule, there's nothing else but grey, meaning that you have achieved everything that has to with the fundraiser and school for the entire day.

You can proceed the same way with audio reminder where each category is represented by a specific ringtone.

- From 8 a.m. to 10 a.m. you have one ringtone.

- At 10:30 a.m. you set another one.

- By 12:00 p.m. you will then set a third ringtone because you are starting with another category.

So it's 3 ringtones for the 3 categories that you've picked; and make sure to set it so as to differentiate them when they mix with one another.

Pinpoint Your Optimal Work Time

Let's try working with another example.

Imagine that you are a writer, and that you have a hard time organizing yourself. You work late, because you wake up late, and before you start writing you have other things to do, like eating, cleaning and possibly working out. You also have to check your mail, or anything else besides writing, which is normal since writing requires a lot of concentration and it can be difficult to stop if you hit a flow with your writing.

Hence, as a writer your problem here is to wake up earlier and set a work-plan that would help you write with a fresher mindset, like around 9 or 10 p.m. instead of 12 p.m. (unless you are a very experienced writer, that's not always the best time, especially for people who manage households or other activities).

Nevertheless, the main priority is writing. But note that, for you to write effectively there must be no "obstruction."

- First things first, get rid of any activity that might prevent you from concentrating. Start your morning by dealing with whatever has to be done in the house, like cleaning, eating breakfast, entertaining your toddler, etc.

- Second, read your emails, check your mailbox, pay some bills, etc.

- Finally, start writing.

Here you have a different setting than the first example because you are organizing your time so that there are no conflicts between the different activities: you first eliminate what can cause obstruction (cleaning and reading emails, etc.), in order to have a more conducive environment for writing with those minor obligations freed from you mind.

Your schedule should be presented as followed on your organizer:

Instant Time Management

Monday 01-20-2015

8-00	-Wake up
8-30	-Clean
9-00	-Clean
9-30	-Clean
10-00	-Workout
10-30	-Workout
11-00	-Workout
11-30	-Check mail box and read your e-mails
12-00	-Eat Lunch
12-30	-Lunch
13-00	-Watch TV
13-30	-TV
14-00	-TV
14-30	-Spend some time with your family
15-00	-family time
15-30	-family time
16-00	-family time.
16-30	-Start writing
17-00	-writing
17-30	-writing
18-00	-writing
18-30	-writing
19-00	-Writing
19-30	-Writing
20-00	-Dinner
20-30	-A short TV break
21-00	-Writing
21-30	-Writing
22-00	-Go to bed

Here you have 3 hours to organize yourself in terms of cleaning, working out and so on (**in yellow**). Then you have activities that have to do with getting updates like reading emails, checking the mailbox, maybe paying a couple of bills (**in green**), and then you can opt for a few hours spent with your family (**in brown**). Finally, comes the time where you can start your writing (**in blue**).

Note how you end up having 3 to 4 hours of non-stop writing for yourself, until 22-00, which is an acceptable time to go to bed.

Have A One-Year Advance

Let's go through one last example.

Imagine that you are a very busy person throughout the year. You are also trying to save up for a house. You are not a big spender, but then comes the end of the year and all the projects you've worked so hard on, start crumbling down.

You are either never ready financially for Christmas, you end up being sick because you work too hard always giving a 100% , but never managing to have some time for yourself or even rest a little; in other words, all work and no play with nothing to show for it!

Well, maybe it's time for you to create some space for fun, and manage your time a bit better. So your first priority, *of course*, is **work**, then **personal projects**, and last your **breaks** during the year.

Moral is, you need to add up some space for leisure or relaxations to help you with your time management schedule.

Here's how your monthly schedule can look like.

2015 Calendar

January	February	March	April	May	June
-Week1: Work	-Week1: Work	-Week1: Work	-Week1: Work	-Week1: Work	-Week1: Work
-Week2 : Work	-Week2: Work	-Week2: work	-Week2: Work	-Week2: Work	-Week2: Work
-Week3 : Work	-Week3: Work	-Week3: Work	-Week3: Work	-Week3: Work	-Week3: Work
-Week4 : Work	-Week4 : Work	-Week4: Work	-Week4: Work		-Week4: Work

July	August	September	October	November	December
-Week1: Work	-Week1: Work	-Week1: Work	-Week1: Work	-Week1: Work	-Week1: Work
-Week2: Work	-Week2: Work	-Week2: Work	-Week2: Work	-Week2: Work	-Week2: Work
-Week3: Work	-Week3: Work	-Week3: Work	-Week3: Work	-Week3: Work	
-Week4: Work	-Week4: Work	-Week4: Work	-Week4: Work	-week4: Work	

This type of advanced planning is for those who are very busy with their work, but it's also suitable for full-time students or stay-at-home moms who have so much to do.

This serves as an example, but work can be substituted with study/class or anything else that keeps you very busy during the year.

To conclude, when presented this way, your calendar tells you when you should take a break during the year (**in orange**). Everything **in blue** is dedicated strictly to your everyday activity (or activities) and everything **in orange** is dedicated to leisure or time-outs during the year.

This way, you have enough space for work or school, etc. and enough space for breaks too, so you don't burn yourself out.

Additionally, this way of organizing yourself (on a weekly basis) is suitable for those who have problems resting during weekends who are stressed about work or just feel that weekends are too short to take a well-deserved break.

<u>Exercise</u>: Start Smart Scheduling

Now, do the following exercise, before moving on to the next section.

1.) Organize your first day of the week. Set the priorities, and color code them.

2.) Secondly, organize your weekly activities for the year (considering that your days will be centered on a single activity).When will be the best time for you to take a break during the year? Explain.

3.) How many times would you envisage taking a break? Explain.

Chapter 6

Evaluating the Effectiveness of Your Time Management

Measure Your Effectiveness

Now that you know how to schedule your game-plan (daily, weekly and yearly) in order to evaluate the time duration and prioritization, let's learn how to control or measure the effectiveness of your time management.

It is crucial that at the end of the day you consult with your organizer to see if you succeeded in completing your activities for that following day, week and so on.

However, this time, instead of doing it at the end of the day, it should be done somewhere during the implementation process, ideally when you are halfway done. But how do you know that you are halfway there?

It's simple, you divide or draw a line separating your schedule in two equal parts.

So if you have to be active for eight hours during the day, divide the 8 hours in two, and then check what you have already done (by looking at all the activities that go above your line or during the first 4 hours).

To Know If Progressing Or Not

<u>Objective</u>: The aim of this activity is to see if you are progressing and to test the effectiveness of how you are managing your time.

The same principle applies to your yearly schedule, where an evaluation should start by the sixth month. This is important because not only does it allow you to know or evaluate your progress, but it also tells you what you need to change in terms of the speed of your implementation.

Don't neglect this step. See it as similar to those step-by-step online tutorials where you are learning to make furniture and must follow the instructions with a lot of attention.

Well, control in time management works the same way. You need to look back and check what you've accomplished, so that you don't ruin the end result where every little step counts.

Exercise: Divide And Evaluate

Do the following exercise.

1.) Set up a new schedule for the year, starting from the very first hour when you are being active to when you go to bed (a sort of daily routine).

2.) Then draw a monthly schedule that goes on for the next 12 months to come.

3.) Now, divide your two schedules so that the timing of your activities are symmetrical (divided in 2 equal time frames).

Now answer the following questions:

- Is separating your schedule in two equal time frames effective for you? Explain.

- Is it easier for you to conduct your daily activities, when using this method? Explain.

Chapter 7
Optimizing Difficult Tasks in Your Schedule for Effective Time Management

Check Off Or Cross Off

After dividing your schedule in half, the next step would be to **check mark** *what has been accomplished* or **cross mark** *what hasn't been accomplished.*

This seems basic, but a lot of people neglect the utilization of these two "tools." These tools, will help you see what needs to be rescheduled. But you don't reschedule these activities on the same day.

It's almost like taking an exam, where you only take into consideration the correct answers, and the wrong ones are eliminated...but saved for another day.

So don't stress about these "failed activities" (if you really look at them like that), considering that you are not made of steel and wires (like a robot), you might not always have enough time to complete a task, pay a bill, or even go to work.

Live To Fight Another Die

Keep in mind that there could be weak links in your schedule, but you can reorganize it for later on during the week.

The bottom line is, you don't want to be disrupted, or ruin your time management because you are trying to catch up with an activity that took too long to complete or, conversely, you insist on rigidly adhering to your schedule to the letter even though time is running out.

Give yourself a chance, and save it for the next day, or postpone for a more appropriate day and time.

After you've rescheduled these cross marked activities, don't forget to use color coding, where you should be using a different color than the ones already used for the different categories of activities. This way, you are warned (by this particular color) that these activities were supposed to be completed earlier during the week, month, or year and that more emphasis is needed on them now.

<u>Exercise</u>: Reschedule Optimization

Think about a time-consuming task or activity on your schedule (the one that you have trouble completing most of the time).

Now think about how you can optimize your schedule to make this activity less of a problem, it can be a few hours on Saturday morning, or 30 minutes of your break-time during the next 3 days, etc. (Use color coding for these missed or failed activities.)

1.) Is this way of optimizing your schedule practical? Explain

2.) Do you better understand the concept of time management up to this point? Explain.

Chapter 8

Daily Nightly Habits for Effective time Management

Plan Your Next Day

It is the end of your day, and you've already checked half your daily routine earlier. Now it's time to check the other half of it, and plan your next day, with the same concept.

Here's what you should set up as a habit: always plan your next day a few hours before bed.

Why? The day is over. You are about to get yourself into bed, yet during the few hours spent at home after returning from work, school, *etc.*, you've had enough time to think about what needs to be done - assuming the same schedule applies daily, or if you want to add or subtract anything from it to make the implementation better, or if you need to go back and do anything that you couldn't get to do earlier

Thus, at the end of the day it should be about following up the same routine every day, or making any necessary changes before the next day.

You Are the Boss And Assistant

Here, you are handling your schedule like an assistant, who always makes sure her boss is updated with the right files, the right information, etc. So keep this in mind; a schedule should be handled with the same manner as a personal assistant, where nothing goes through the "CEO," unless you've checked that "these files" they're all good.

The same principle can be applied to your New Year's resolution, when you look over the past year and see if there's anything you could improve, etc.

For example, at this time of year you can check the list of all your accomplishments during the past year against your last year list of resolutions. Then you can evaluate why you haven't done certain things, what has worked and what hasn't, and mostly take into consideration the reasons why you maybe didn't function optimally this last year (it could be stress, or some unpredictable events). This gives you the opportunity remedy these flaws during the new year.

Always remember to be positive when setting up your schedule. Positivity can also give you good ideas for a good schedule.

<u>Exercise</u>: Daily Progress Equates Yearly Success

1.) Draw a daily routine, think about what you should add to make it more effective (consider time framing here and the number of activities).

2.) Do the same with your yearly resolution this time. Think about what you hope to accomplished last year. Think about how you should organize yourself daily, weekly (even hourly) to make this new year smoother and make your life easier.

The purpose of this exercise is for you to see what needs to be done daily for your year to be a success (energy and objective wise).

Chapter 9

Exercises for Effective time Management

Exercise 1: Test Your Understanding

Answer the following questions:

1.) Time management, is about applying the "time is money" principle.
a.) True
b.) False

2.) Time management is closely linked to organizing yourself around a daily mechanism based around a time

frame, the respect of that time frame and a good evaluation technique of the implementation process.

a.) True

b.) False

3.) As long as you respect your daily routine, time management should be an easy concept for you.

a.) True

b.) False

<u>Exercise 2</u>: Create Your Schedules

Set a very personalized and concise schedule for yourself. Use the reminder tools that suit you best (color coding, alarm, ring tone, or come up with your own).

Next, do the same for your **weekly schedule** (including the weekend). And then your **yearly schedule**.

Take <u>5 minutes</u> and have a look at all of them.

1.) Do you feel that your schedule is realistic enough? Explain.

2.) If yes, what would be the things you would add or subtract to make it more effective? Explain (proceed by meticulously envisioning going through your hourly routine).

Exercise 3: Assimilate All The Tools

According to you, what pushes people to ruin their daily schedule? Explain. What would be a solution here. Be very application-based with your answer. You can explain how color coding or other reminders help; also think about the different steps to follow in time management.

Write your answer in a **minimum of 300 words**. The purpose here, is to see if you have assimilated the steps to follow and the importance of using reminders.

Exercise 4: Synergize What Works

According to you, what should motivate somebody to take a break yearly? Should a break during a year be motivated by following the same rhythm (in term of routine) as anybody else or by hard work supported by a solid, personalized and a well thought-out schedule?

Answer this question by comparing the non-methodic routines with more elaborated ones in **300 words**.

Chapter 10
No Tasks Left Behind for Effective Time Management

Follow Through Your Schedule

Finally, we've come to our last but important chapter. How do you remember to follow up on an activity?

First, you were told how to reschedule one, but now you should explore the techniques to help you with remembering. With time management, memory is also important.

To start, use the reminder tools. They are great instant visual aids and good for color coding. For example, as soon as you open your organizer, assigning a specific color to write down an activity for 10 o'clock can be very useful.

Let's not forget (as mentioned earlier), that a different color should be used for **rescheduled activities** because they becomes a different priority (depending on the way it's color coded), helping you remember faster because it attracts your attention, as soon as you open up your organizer to a specific day.

Time Management Chart

Our next method, for effective memory, is the use of **time a management chart.** You should be able to make one that measures the implementation of each category.

At the end of the day, you should quickly draw a chart that represents the different categories of activities. If you've completed all your activities for the day, the chart should tell you this by putting all the activities on the same level; but if one category has a lot of incomplete activities, it should also be portrayed in the chart.

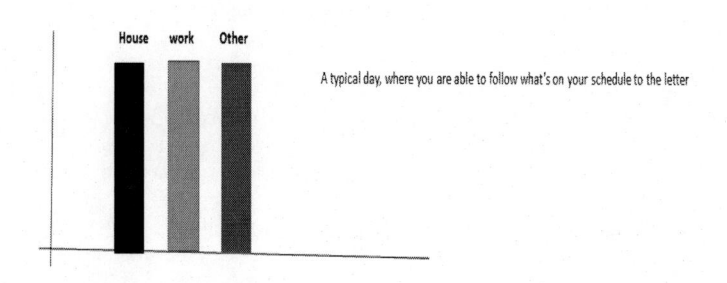

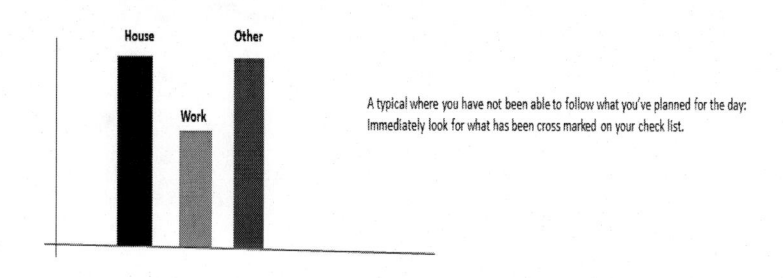

A typical day, where you are able to follow what's on your schedule to the letter

A typical where you have not been able to follow what you've planned for the day: Immediately look for what has been cross marked on your check list.

Here you have an example of a time management chart where <u>3 categories</u> of activities are being represented, namely: house, work and other.

- The first graph shows you a successfully implemented schedule.

- The second one in turn, shows you that a lot of your activities linked to your work, haven't been completed yet.

What happens is that, whenever one of the graphs (or more) is not at the same level as the others, you should consult your checklist, immediately. It's a simple process, it only takes a few minutes (whether on paper or electronically). It's very practical and allows you be have a more interactive schedule.

This should be done a couple of minutes before bed, every night, before scheduling your next day. Now isn't this a great way to manage your time effectively so that you never lose focus on what needs to be done,?

Another bonus with this technique is that it might be the last thing you register in your mind every day. Now you will wake up the next day, having the color and shapes of your graphs in your head, thinking to yourself: *"Weren't those shoes on the left shelf supposed to be delivered yesterday?"*

Implementation Table

Another useful tool would be an **implementation table** that tells you what needs to be done like an organizer, but the good thing is you can create one whenever you want. It doesn't have to be fancy, it's just a table where you write what you have to do during the day, to help you with your memory. It is a good tool because, you don't always have your organizer with you or you can forget to take your phone when you go on a break (these things happen all the time), so a little implementation table can come in handy here.

Here you have an example of an implementation table (very basic).

1- Important client to pick at airport	9-......
2- Make a cake for son	
3-Birthday bash for friend	
4-Car repair	
5-Call client at 4h30	
6-Lunch with the boss	
7-Must finish wiring report today...	
8-...	

You don't need to write the time down, just the different activities, because its purpose is simply to help refresh your memory on what's written in your schedule for the day. So keep it with you, and consult it whenever you need to make sure you are doing the right thing.

Do you ever have those moments when you feel like you are forgetting to do something, or you feel like things are just moving too smoothly for the day? Well, this implementation table can help you deal with those moments of doubts.

You can even make one at the end of your day, when you are feeling tired and you just don't feel like doing anything. All you want is to lay down and sleep. Well, this implementation table can help you here, as you simply write down all that you've completed for the day on a piece of paper or phone, and leave it like that for the next day.

The next day, you know *what you've accomplished* and *what you didn't*. This could be considered as a last resort, for time management of the next day, since you are already feeling tired.

There! We've gone through some very useful tips to help you follow up your activities the next day.

<u>Exercise</u>: Use Last Minute Chart

Do this last and final exercise.

1.) Pick a number of categories (at most 4), that make up your activities.

2.) Which ones are easier to complete, and which ones are not? Explain.

3.) How would you use a time management chart to represent them? Explain.

Chapter 11
The Time to Start Effective Time Management is NOW

More Times Are Wasted Than Ever

Effective time management is an issue for a lot of people. As the years pass, it would appear as though the issue has worsened.

Looking closely, you may even come up with the conclusion that our grandparents were the masters at following their everyday routines, even though there were perhaps no sophisticated gadgets, or tools to help them out.

They got things done with discipline and all these other values that we have abandoned, throughout the years.

Now that doesn't mean that you work with less passion or determination today; it probably means that you are less organized because things seem easier.

Finding a way to manage time can lead to headaches and unpleasantries, for most of us, and you can't disagree with that. There's not enough time to rest, not enough time to close a deal with a client, and so on.

Sometimes you just want to give up, because it just seems that there's never enough time for anything. And this is one thing that technology can't provide us with: a way to manage time better. Technology doesn't manage time for us; we only use it as a tool to manage time for us.

Time Management Is Just Self-Management

So arm yourself with the appropriate tools and follow the steps to a more effective time management process

You've probably thought about it or said it every day that you need to be more organized or you need to manage your time more effectively, yet the process doesn't have to be boring. You can get as creative and sophisticated as possible to how you do so, such as using ringtones as reminders or being inventive with color coding.

The bottom line is, you need to get started with a good daily or weekly schedule that will help you manage YOURSELF more easily.

Forget time management; it should be self-management! Time can not be controlled. It will always keep going; however, we always have the option to control ourselves.

No time to waste. Time to get started now!

Instant Time Management

An INSTANT Thank You!

Thank you for entrusting in the INSTANT Series to help you improve your life.

Our goal is simple, help you achieve instant results as fast as possible in the quickest amount of time. We hope we have done our job, and you have gotten a ton of value.

If you are in any way, shape, or form, dissatisfied, then please we encourage you to get refunded for your purchase because we only want our readers to be happy.

If, *on the other hand*, you've enjoyed it, if you can kindly leave us a review on where you have purchased this book, that would mean a lot.

What is there to do now?

Simple! Head over to http://www.instantseries.com, and sign up for our **newsletter** to stay up-to-date with the latest instant developments *(if you haven't done so already)*.

Be sure to check other books in the INSTANT Series. If there is something you like to be added, be sure to let us know for as always we love your feedback.

Yes, we're on **social medias.** *Don't forget to follow us!*

https://www.facebook.com/InstantSeries

https://twitter.com/InstantSeries

https://plus.google.com/+Instantseries

Thank you, and wish you all the best!
- *The INSTANT Series Team*

Instant Time Management

Manufactured by Amazon.ca
Acheson, AB